Resurrection of the Mannequins

Resurrection of the Mannequins

Poems by

Ruth Towne

© 2025 Ruth Towne. All rights reserved.
This material may not be reproduced in any form, published,
reprinted, recorded, performed, broadcast,
rewritten, or redistributed without
the explicit permission of Ruth Towne.
All such actions are strictly prohibited by law.

Cover design by Shay Culligan
Cover image by Daria Gordova on Unsplash
Author photo by Sarah La Croix Photography

ISBN: 978-1-63980-730-7

Kelsay Books
502 South 1040 East, A-119
American Fork, Utah 84003
Kelsaybooks.com

Acknowledgments

Many thanks to the editors of the following publications where these poems first appeared, sometimes in alternate versions:

Afflatus Apparatus: "Observatory Time, the Lovers"
The Afterpast Review: "Siren Stars Alice"
Anodyne Review: "The Vet and the Bull"
Arboreal Literary Magazine: "M@rcəl Jə@n's Mannequin"
Assignment Literary Magazine: "J°@n M!r°'s Mannequin," "Exquisite Corpse #05"
BarBar Literary Magazine: "Nahui Olín at a Bullfight"
Broken Antler Magazine: "S@lv@d°r D@ll's Mannequin"
Coffin Bell Journal: "Lə° M@lət's Mannequin," "M@n R@y's Mannequin"
The Decadent Review: "Tanja Ramm under a Bell Jar"
foofaraw: "Seventh Peril"
Gyroscope Review: "°sc@r D°m!ngЦəz's Mannequin"
Holy Gossip: "The Years Lie in Wait for You"
In Parentheses: "KЦrt Səl!gm@nn's Mannequin," "@ndrə M@ss°n's Mannequin," "Exquisite Corpse #04," "Experimental Research," "The Lovers"
Lily Poetry Review: "W°lfg@ng P@@lən's Mannequin"
The Listening Eye: "M@Цr!cə Hənry's Mannequin"
Luxury Literature: "Exquisite Corpse #03"
Malu Zine: "Gloria de Herrera, Saint-Martin d'Ardèche, France"
Midway Journal: "Girl with Death Mask"
miniMAG: "M@rcəl DЦch@mp's Mannequin," "Portrait of Space"
Neologism Poetry Review: "Lost Object"
New Feathers Anthology: "Resurrection of the Mannequins"
New Note Poetry: "Sea and Sunshine"
Paranoid Tree: "Ecstatic Cow"

Poor Ezra's Almanac: "Given: 1. The Waterfall, 2. The Illuminating Gas," "Yvǝs T@ngⅡy's Mannequin"
Quibble Quarterly: "Surrealist Games"
redrosethorns: "Decalcomania with River and Bridge," "Minotaur"
Scud: "X-ray of My Skull," "Yobi-goe (The Call)"
Stonecoast Literary Review: "Ǝsp!n°z@'s Mannequin"
TXTOBJX: "Surrealist Inquiry"
Weaver Magazine: "Exquisite Corpse #02"

Contents

[1]

Resurrection of the Mannequins	19
Exquisite Corpse #03	21
KUrt Səl!gm@nn's Mannequin	24
M@x Ǝrnst's Mannequin	25
Ecstatic Cow	27
Surrealist Games	28
@ndrə M@ss°n's Mannequin	29
Exquisite Corpse #02	30
S°n!@ M°ssə's Mannequin	33
Decalcomania with River and Bridge	34
Lə° M@lət's Mannequin	41

[2]

Yobi-goe (The Call)	45
M@rcəl Jə@n's Mannequin	46
Tanja Ramm Under a Bell Jar	50
Sea and Sunshine	52
S@lv@d°r D@l!'s Mannequin	53
Surrealist Inquiry	54
J°@n M!r°'s Mannequin	55
Seventh Peril	59
M@Ur!cə Hənry's Mannequin	60
Exquisite Corpse #01	62
Gloria de Herrera, Saint-Martin d'Ardèche, France	63
The Weaver of Verona	65
Lost Object	75

[3]

From Another Approach	79
W°lfg@ng P@@lən's Mannequin	82
Experimental Research	83
Exquisite Corpse #04	84
M@rcəl DUch@mp's Mannequin	85
Nahui Olín at a Bullfight	86
The Lovers	87
Yvəs T@ngUy's Mannequin	88
°sc@r D°m!ngUəz's Mannequin	89
The Vet and the Bull	90

[4]

Əsp!n°z@'s Mannequin	93
Girl with Death Mask	96
X-ray of My Skull	97
M@n R@y's Mannequin	98
Portrait of Space	100
The Years Lie in Wait for You	101
Minotaur	102
Exquisite Corpse #05	104
Observatory Time, the Lovers	105
Siren Stars Alice	110
Given: 1. The Waterfall, 2. The Illuminating Gas	112
Notes	115

What does Breton ask of the most clear-sighted spirits of our time? Nothing less than the courage to embark on an adventure which—who knows?—may well prove fatal, but from which one can hope—and that is what is essential—to attain the total conquest of the mind.

—Suzanne Césaire, *1943: Surrealism and Us*

[1]

Resurrection of the Mannequins

Mirror-clear water bisects me as I rise
from under its polished surface. Above,
the moon is a jellyfish, a neon night light.
It hovers, that umbrella with its tentacles

in fuchsia, blue, and magenta. Before this,
I was a girl who grew to life in the water,
a champagne glass curved and crystalline.
Not far from here, I think I hear a woman

scream, but her fear is music, siren's song.
And how strange, if once there were stars
above me I can't recall. Maybe they hanged
there while clouds concealed them, ordinary

like green fruits of ornamental apple trees.
Once, I was younger longer than expected.
And once, I had ideas of who I'd live to be.
I have a fragment of an idea, an impression

of a dream. Each orb substitutes for a star,
and it's not the dream itself but a memory
of the dream, a particle of light arriving light
years later, an ancient light that passes on.

On shore, a handful of crystal figurines turn
on pointed toes, dancing under fluorescents,
those beautiful music box-bound ballerinas,
those exquisite dead in blush pink leotards.

They store their deaths in those music boxes.
On command the dancers turn. They assemblé.
They pirouette. Elsewhere, other dancers wait
their turns, passé. Once, they were becoming.

Now, no one speaks of them. Here, a headless
woman and the head of a woman are equal,
and no one can stomach one whole. Violence
is a commodity, a tiny tchotchke as common

as a half-shell on any beach, bleach-white,
ready for collection. Later, a crowd will feed
on my bare body—I, the ever-lovely carrion;
they, the rock-brown lobsters scavenging

a bouldered ocean floor. Somewhere close,
a melancholy melody swells, a hollow blow
of a nautilus shell follows. I know the song.
It's welcoming me home to this far harbor

where the sea is dahlia blue and the medusa
moon pulses like a burnt nerve. It's my turn
—somewhere, there's a music box for me.
In another life, I dreamed I was a ballerina.

Exquisite Corpse #03

                        enter the maze
                     in dull gray shades

in the brain where it begins

in dew like glass tears
and golden heather, crickets, croaking toads
I stand barefoot in the grass
         the earth is hard and charged

                I'll answer questions now
once I am ready to die
I want to quiet my own mind
I hollow myself out from the inside

         a bare polar bear rug
         a reclining nude
the grotto of my body, spring fed

an artist's time comes after her death
and so it goes with muses

                    the days are shorter
                   the earth rotates faster
              a leap day left off the calendar

imagine, I am desperate to be forgotten
imagine, I have no way to make my name

                        empty snakeskin
                      empty turtle shell

imagine, the air is humid
with music of other muses

I just want quiet
        salt in water, snapdragon,
                foxglove, the burning eye

imagine, stones to my feet,
                boots over my shoulder
tied together, fingers laced
        glacier, river, water flows
        cold slate stones

                        I feel the earth
the river, it snakes like an eel

shade of an elm tree
daisies in a flowerbed
a croquet mallet to the head

        if water can only reach the sea
solvent of life, dissolved in all

root of evil
box of dog bones

given the choice I would carve
                the thing out from myself
                    the part that needs

in the garden, barefoot in grass and shadow

      who is not looking for a reason
      but there is no one reason

   it is difficult for me to say what I mean
once and for all, plain

I want quiet in my own mind
      to rush across crushed stone
            no matter how hard or sharp

      underfoot it never hurts, the earth
once, it never hurts

KUrt Səl!gm@nn's Mannequin

How beautifully you bruised when your collarbone split, before calcium carbonate bound to bone. The tissue grew back scar-hard and carbon-dark. A solitary polyp bloomed, then one polyp became two. I saw the secret reef pulsing between your bones. And you showed me where it hurt.

Once, I was a doll in emerald waters. Don't you remember? Now, I adorn myself in drowned women's jewels and lost fishing nets. A shoulder blade breaks away, another reef grows on a statue cast under the sea. You must remember— you and I are ends of one bone that never healed whole.

M@x Ǝrnst's Mannequin

Cider Mill Hill curves like a terminal nerve,
and below, below, below, its old asphalt cracks

then creases, a blanket the years have worn well
and torn between pale and dark green squares.
It is August ten years ago, in the way some past

summers are never more and never less than ten
years away, in the way some memories remain

bright and excursive, small solstices in the mind.
At rigid plank's end, she stands on her maple-made
longboard, steady. She stares down that steep road,

its flocks of tender hemlocks blocking either edge,
its rust-colored pine needles lining a steep shoulder,

a throw of red-evergreen to blanket the roadside.
On this afternoon in August ten years ago, she has
the certain nerve that tells the brain to tell the body,

Go, this is your moment. So she pushes off, down
the hill, sense and synapse, lost in her body now.

* * *

It is pain she never repeats, an ache decaying long.
In her body, she holds all else as long as she can,
the one who sees her fall and helps her up again,

the jeans, light wash and with a gash at the knee,
the slate gray breaks in the stone-hard road,

the longboard in the trough of Cider Mill Hill.
Lost equinox of easy living, the body holds it all—
the way back to the eroding road, the hurt, the nerve.

Ecstatic Cow

Ceramic cows come out of the ground like flowers. It is late November as they rise in the milk-quiet twilight. They move together clanging. They are all hollow objects. Each time one strikes into the side of another, they make sounds like cowbells tied around so many cows' necks. One by one, I herd them inside. First, come figurines in black, brown, and white. Each time I reach inside the tiny China cabinet, I see myself inside, in the mirror behind, the way my grandmother saw herself when her mother gave her these figurines. One muscular red bull stops with me. Its gold speckled neck, its gilt horns and hooves are bright as sunlight moving over earth. I say, *Sir, who belongs to whom?* Then come figures with brindling, and in cream, pastel, painted with daisies, wearing flower crowns. A cow with a black hide and cold blue eyes arrives. It sits like a dog. It is leashed in gold to two small calves, her to each and each to her. I say, *Please, Madam, do I love you because someone I love also loved someone who loved you?* Then come the roan gravy boat, the crushed velvet bobble head lowering itself to graze, the gray ashtray, the tall baby bottle. I behold everything my family leaves for me, real and unreal, these figurines once bouquet bright now decaying, passing with the light into shades of gray. So many cows are crowding around. I cannot see a way out. And more await me outside my window. They keep rising out of the ground and off into the moonlight. I am moonstruck by the menagerie. Then comes a cow with its thorax pocked, a lunar surface, another heirloom, another moon. I ask, *Do I keep you?* And now I do, the way one keeps any family secret.

Surrealist Games

Elizabeth Short: When the dark and carbon-hard pavement
curves during the rain,
Black Dahlia: I become aware of my own breathing each
morning before morning.

Black Dahlia: When I hear fingers drumming faint
and impatient on window panes,
Elizabeth Short: mist and spray make the street mirror me,
a temporary looking glass.

Black Dahlia: If I try to feel the lines inside me, the places
where my seams conjoin,
Elizabeth Short: the water knows where to go, it seeks its own,
in drains, in vapor.

Elizabeth Short: If my neighbor had not hanged her socks
on the clothesline last night,
Black Dahlia: this awareness is a distorted form of immortality
for us insomniacs.

Elizabeth Short: When I am upside-down in atmosphere, double-
exposed here in air,
Black Dahlia: I keep on living inside my head,
as of yet I cannot escape any lower.

@ndrə M@ss°n's Mannequin

What is real?
And who's to say?

Once, you came back
    down Cerise Street,
under lamplight glow,
    in the gloaming hour
    and autumn's bronze,

you were a frame of silk stretched,
you were blank mesh under tension.

White gold, the copper red
    you said you loved,
then goldenrod again—

    when one lamp blinks out,
    you will find her,
who you are
    whoever you are

a spot of charcoal, a blot of ink—
    then, you will have your answers.

Exquisite Corpse #02

a pebble, a hook—
        in other people's memory
                I tuck myself away
      just around the other side
             of consciousness

          a pleasant thought,
             that you can walk away, apart
      and someone might keep you
so the reverse: your backs turn,
to never think of you again

     a thought   so small
never even
            a pebble

      a dream is not desire, it's recognition
      there's another looking, too

          there's a cord
     in the telephone
it coils   the years
     it descends
         to a black block

        I slip into myself
like a summer sundress,
     all sewed out
of peony petals
areola rosy
hymen delicate

I grew a freckle   —a pebble, a hook—
          in my eye

follow the lines from my mouthpiece
to your mouth, the hook of the phone
a dream but not a desire
recognition before passion   recognition

        I have come to adore
the back of your head
        man and woman
        with their faces obscured
the son of man, the lady and the bird

                        I have forgotten
                              how to sleep
                    I am content to forget
        I'm awake
how difficult   to prove a lack

        I have long known about myself
there is a trap door I am desperate to spring
the trigger lies with you, a silver hook—

yes   I see you   yes, I see
                              you've carried
                    a pebble
with you
        these years

      first desire, then separation
                          not passion
next recognition
              there   was desire—

it would be a kindness if you remembered
it would be a marvel if you searched for

      a pebble—a hook—

you say, yes, I'll be back   soon

—how difficult to prove a lack

S°n!@ M°ssə's Mannequin

in seablack in mist & whispers
in a garden of wax roses
arises the empire of light

i outlived myself once
but no one can outrun that storm gorgeous eye
forever, that rocky body in solar orbit
it soars above a forest of stars
a diamond egg waxing bloodblue

each spring, i eat my evil
in the blush of the communion cup,
in the rinds of sliced lemons and limes,
in rainraw honey lathered into sweet rust
in the forms of spiders that slide into one's mouth at night

what good would it do to admit that i'm sick?
i heave the moon—that large pink petal—
into the waters of the night
it floats slow in the lake of the sky
a lost blossom

i hope i can outlive myself again,
in spite of my instincts

purple and black, wax rose petals shine back night
it's a light as light as seaspray
i surrender to the morning star
& the summer in me aches away

Decalcomania with River and Bridge

Over the railing of the bridge
below me but not so far, a river

disintegrates, it comes to an end
of sorts, it throws itself over,

over, into the ravine of serrate rocks,
irregular teeth at the river's mouth.

Once, my husband demonstrates
how little it takes as we visit.

We stand together at the edge
looking below. I am warm in summer sun.

Vapor takes shape in the air after a storm.
I listen as he explains, I am still as water,

tranquil, as if on each of my daily visits
as I walk the road beside this river

I don't consider going over,
which he doesn't know.

Water releases water as drops,
body releases body as thought—

misting up, sinking down, in the air,
on the rocks. Water, body separate,

are separate, come together again.
I have wondered over this edge

of water times before. Once, I am five
inside the glossy shell of a green canoe

when I ride over inside my mind.
I try to stop then. A horizontal board

out of view makes that water's edge,
a boundary somewhere under the water

for the water's surface to sublimate,
to suppress. Bless the board, it holds me

from going over, however invisibly.
Here, the rail is thigh-high, perpendicular,

green as liberty, as the old canoe I keep
in my mind. All this—the bridge, the river

below the bridge, the cliff below the river
—all this waits for me. All this passes

a vacant mill graying, deteriorating.
That building lists toward water's edge.

It does not remember what it was like
when its turbines first turned. But the river

remembers how it surged before the dam.
I am behind the rail at the bridge's edge.

As is its habit, the bridge keeps practiced
in the air. As is my tendency, I visit here

to look at the river decomposing below.
So this is how I see myself go over:

first the bridge rail, head heavy, thoughtless
then thoughts lost in the air. In the air—

I hang there as long as possible,
suspended, pendant and pendent.

Since the bridge is not so high,
there is hardly time for me

to digress, to wonder between edge
of bridge and edge of water at the quiet

while the river lulls by, a music box
unwinding in dead air. For an instant

I am below the river below the bridge
as water catches me. It deadens

my fall. Then I float again, face to the base
of the bridge, flat on my back, in the black

and turbid current, feeling first
since I hanged there in the air

the changed way my body makes sense
of the water, how I can sense more

than temperature and pressure there,
how my body does not guess at sensation.

I feel what someone always ought to feel,
what the water ought to feel like now,

how water always was without me.
So afloat and knowing what going over

is like, then I could find the river's edge
and climb out of the water,

and back to my senses again,
or maybe

I could stay floating almost over,
or not.

Of course, there are other bridges to go
over. I am ten when I come to know

a strange chain-weighted bridge
by its name, *Memorial*. Before this,

I name each bridge by its unique
feature or shape: *Pillar, Mill, Metal Grate,*

Four-Square, and *Dinosaur,* that high
and ancient frame scaled patina-green

and towering over the river-harbor's mouth.
Then, at seventeen, I am driving over

that dinosaur, when I consider
pure distance—

White Mountains bounding the west,
Atlantic constraining the east,

all that water and air beneath me,
and I think to myself, *Hold tight. Hold tight.*

Here, not far off from bridge and river,
maples and pine trees cling to the riverside

as the river erodes rocks and boulders
leftover from ancient glaciers.

This landscape lives while I do.
It changes. It decays.

I have carried the image of the river
and the bridge with me all my life.

And I remember what it is like
with my father behind me

in the green canoe at the edge,
how surely the current will take us away,

how despite my crying he goes forward
pressing his oar toward the empty place

where the water falls
because it cannot go.

He keeps rowing.
Bless him, he keeps rowing.

Below me, the river deteriorates
the day my husband demonstrates going

where the bridge rail splits,
where the two sides of the bridge seam.

He slides easily, rainwater in a stream
between those pillars. He holds himself over

for an instant. And he considers it,
the plunge under into wet leaves and rotten

waterlogged branches in silt and mud.
When he returns from his odyssey

between the beams, he explains to me
what held him inside,

this expansion joint, a design
for the bridge to breathe.

Then he points below the other side
of the rail. He shows me the concrete

pillar of the bridge to which he swims,
his point of return in the current.

It's my turn, so I point to a tiny horizon,
where the water falls

over the dam's wood ledge,
where beside, a ladder rises

at the last moment
as I am back to the bridge

and the river, eye to the mist
as it rises up, sunk close to under

the water as it throws itself over,
where I am so close to going.

Bless it. Bless this river. Bless this bridge.
Bless this way of living as I go.

Lə° M@lət's Mannequin

The note is a final touch, a preparation for the afterlife,
it will be a small stone amulet between papyrus linens.
But the walls are going up, there is no time to compose
either message or the messenger. Tomorrow it will be

sealed inside the sheetrock, waiting, one would hope,
decades for another stranger to excavate that tomb.
So she finds she's telling the future what anyone would—
who planted the peonies and where the pets are buried.

[2]

Yobi-goe (The Call)

The ocean knows that kind-of silence
she came for. The siren-high view
lures her in. To avoid her disquiet
flooding up, a great hollow breaker,

she came for the siren-high view—
on the coast, ocean foams across rock,
flooding up a great hollow breaker
almost over the balcony's metal edge.

On the coast, ocean foams across rock.
A rogue wave, a surge urges her off
almost over the balcony's metal edge.
The undercurrent, the persistent blue,

a rogue wave, a surge urges her off,
lures her into a void. Her disquiet,
the undercurrent, the persistent blue—
the ocean knows that kind of silence.

M@rcəl Jə@n's Mannequin

Atlantic Avenue, Virginia Beach, Virginia

All saline and aquamarine, a warm wave sways me.
I lay back in the Atlantic as a friend and I drift apart.

With half the world to my bare back, I rest. The rest
is all west. I crack the universe in two, a bivalve shell

in brackish swells. Everywhere, strangers wade or play
while I float away. Back on shore, the soft sand shrieks

sun back to the light. Across the smooth quartz dune,
dozens of umbrellas swell, cool cerulean medusae.

And inland, almost far away, scores of other tourists
escape the sweltering street, sheltering as they can

among mannequins in air-conditioned tchotchke shops.
And I was right earlier when I said, *It's a lovely day*

to fill one's pockets with rocks and walk into the sea.
Earlier, I faced the passenger window as we bobbed

across packed highway lanes, and the black compact
in which we rode was another unlucky, slick sardine.

We were on our way to a vacation within a vacation,
to a break within a break. We were silent as stones

until I spoke. It's all becoming clearer now, as I float
here alone. Break by break, the sea carries me away

from shore, toward a sandbar that's been swallowing
smooth swells all day, only to spit them out creased

and foaming white. Nearby, shallow shadows cast
back to a fishing pier its elongated shape. And afar,

dolphins appear—alone, in pairs, alone again. Earlier,
we were destined for a boardwalk and for the beach.

But we arrived to another reality—kiosks and concrete,
a strip mall three miles long, a block of ossified hotels

breaking the coast from view. How long did we tread
that pale plaster desert before I realized that death

is not something to casually reference, no less death
by suicide? And how long until I caught the silence

to follow? Later, I'll consider that quiet an offense,
since my insensitive allusion to Ms. Woolfe's death,

a tragedy, went unrecognized, yet no one stopped me
from visiting this beach. Now the saltwater burns

my eyes. Now the sea alleviates the heat. Now I see many
reasons why one doesn't make light of death by suicide.

It's a lovely day. It was an awful thing to say. On shore,
the sunbathers are mannequins now, bronze and brown

dolls posed far apart while children play in the shade
of empty jellyfish bells. I drift away from my friend.

She waded to shallow water. My landmark, she stands
back-to me on cement-hard sand, while the water hides

her below the waist. I know I tried, but she and I
couldn't swim at the same pace. And on concrete

we did not walk at the same rate, though I swear
I tried to shift my stride. We find ourselves apart.

Later, she'll ask, *What's something you'd change
to alter your current life in some meaningful way?*

She'll answer herself after a break. For her, there's nothing.
Life happened to her and look at what after all it made.

I'll say nothing. She is a doll in the tide. I am the waves.
All around, strange mannequins wear neoprene, spandex,

sometimes sunscreen. All around, figurine fragments wash
away—the arms and legs and heads of dismembered dolls,

those lost toys. Away, my friend waves at me, I wave back.
Later, she'll say, *I love you because you're a lot like me.*

It's a lovely day, so I'll silently disagree. At one time,
experts considered the beach a place of healing. Tumors,

imbalanced humors, even melancholy—all these, a shock
of cold sea could cure. I stare into the bell jar of the sky,

the ultramarine atmosphere. There's no return from here,
no coming back from this beach, this break. So breaks

another wave. I lay back in the Atlantic. I drift away.
Anyway, a beach is nothing more than loose sand shifting,

fluid land one longs to visit but where one cannot stay.
And I was right earlier when I said, *It's a lovely day.*

Tanja Ramm Under a Bell Jar

Before the cloche, she had grown new bone
 out of the side of her right foot. This was due
  to pointed-toe boots, her black suede shoes.

Until recently, she had been content to live
 in a hotel suite, even though the windows
  never opened. Oh those windows, squares

of glass squares above a patio scattered
 with metal chairs cushioned in blue, gray,
  and white, above a half-dozen palm trees

around a portal-shaped swimming pool,
 above a parking lot haunted by white gulls.
  And when her cellphone learned she'd left

the east coast for the west coast, it showed
 her what she'd like to do outside her room:
  hear a string quartet perform by candlelight

in the womb of a Catholic chapel, or visit
 the tomb of a decommissioned submarine,
  or walk through the museum of cannibals,

myth and reality exhibited room by room.
 The phone was right about what she'd like
  to do, and the room was fine. It overlooked

a pool. Perhaps if the window could open
 she would jump feet first into the deep end,
  all four feet of water, then she would swim

from side to side, a rogue typhoon let loose
        on a harbor. But the window stayed closed,
                so she rested on the sill, her slim pedestal.

Soon she grew to hate that stupid hotel room,
        her glass vacuum. When she saw her body cut off
                across a glossy lock screen, she chose the cloche.

She did it for the cellphone and the new bone.
        She welcomed the dome with her eyes closed
                like windows, her lips red, her head severed.

Sea and Sunshine

        impressions of hands

      waves reach
across Ocean Beach

        thin fingers, each ridge
arches whorls loops

     * * *

    slender arch, brittle star
one arm regrows a whole starfish

     * * *

lost week
        whorls loops
     fingerprints in ink

how many more
of me grow
     from me?

S@lv@d°r D@l!'s Mannequin

Stretching out straight like a boa preparing to swallow you—
    at three, you saw a golden asp in its cage at the zoo,
    at thirteen, you twisted your fingers and palms
        into hand shadow snakes, flat and hissing,
    at thirty, you work for a greedy woman.

You write a chapter of her book for her.
You walk her white dog on the sidewalk outside her hotel.
You set her dining table for her,
    place a fork and knife on either side of a coiled anaconda.
You serve dessert, a small deer for the snake inside her to eat.

You attend a party in her honor,
    walk the white dog in the parking lot,
    add another chapter and say, *It's brilliant,*
    what she's written.

You dream her pages are full as a classroom,
    full of machine guns.
    They shine like oil, those noisy toys.
    They recite the alphabet for you, treasured figurines.

You attend a party in her home.
Again, in her home, you review sketches at the kitchen table
    while she fills your water cup,
    while the white dog coils at your feet, an albino snake.

You give your life for her greed, you in the front of her classroom.
You write down a thought on the clock, it belongs to her, too,
    even the one about starting new, before the caged snake,
    even the one in which you are born as one of the guns.

Surrealist Inquiry

I hate treachery of imagination—the philosopher was born behind a door. She left, like some others whose mothers gave birth in closed rooms. How many more will open?—from one door follows every other.

I love water as it plays with light, as though even a small silver spoon could contain a tropical lagoon, a crystal-blue grotto forgotten by all but the sun, as though the light always knew it would be waves, as though I could be, too.

I want God in a looking glass.

I fear I will never see myself. Light transforms, one door opens to another door.

J°@n M!r°'s Mannequin

When the fish first walked
it was October.
I never told.
I had been alone
as one always seems to be
for such unreal wonders.
And it was just one fish
after all, not something more awful
or concrete, a Loch Ness Monster
complete with flattened tail
and pearlescent scales, rising
from its abyssal home
to drag me sunken under
all to its murky glory.

This was simply a fish
with feet,
you would not believe how ordinary,
something even like a sunfish
or slighter,
barely visible to me when it bathed
in daylight, warming
up its blood under sunny waters.
But, I admit I knew it quickly,
the heart of this fish
is half-chambered beside mine.
The blood of this fish runs cold.

So who ought I have told?
Who is qualified to hold
this knowledge with me
without having seen it?
And who would believe me?
And if they believed, then—?

Wouldn't they take me away?
There are only so many places
a person can go with me
with those vestigial feet.

It seems the fish has no plans
to leave me.
It follows along
with its four small feet
each the size of a wet leaf
and leaving webbed prints
I step in
again and again
keeping my feet perpetually wet.

The fish has not slept.
Instead, it has been making
me a kind of ladder
that leans between
our worlds,
its and mine.
The fish wants me
to climb. I think it misses
the like company
of other fishes.
I think it wants to see
what will happen to me
if I go with it.

I never thought I would live
with this fish at all, then so long.

Once, someone nearly caught me,
she was listening then
with a net to her ear.
She detected visions
of mine the fish influenced.
I never admitted
because I did not wish
to be, irrevocably, Fish-Girl,
which is an honorific
one cannot lift once it fits.

And I have not been indifferent.
I have developed ways to coexist.
I can breathe through a wire
impossibly slim.
I fashioned a chamber with air
to swim in.
Just as you did not know
about the fish,
so, I have kept all this
from the fish.

But the fish persists.
This has something to do
with doing things over,
and the yearly greeting
to submarines still on patrol,
and how chalky drawings
of mermaids fade
in autumn rain,
bleeding mint and teal.

So when it completes
its ladder for me, finally,
the fish will be as bright as Christ
as he strides away
on waves on the Sea of Galilee,
and the fish will be foreknowing as Jonah
in the storm as he throws
himself away
into his great whale.
That will be its way of saying,
Come back in. Come back in.
Whether or not I want
to follow, you understand,
the fish will insist,
wading there on four feet
by its unfathomable ladder
that goes immortally lower.

The fish is with me,
but I resist.
With my wire lifeline
and my umbilical and metal bell,
I resist.
And I am admitting all this
because I want to outlive
the miracle fish.

Seventh Peril

                He sees in apple red. I see in dahlia blue.
This theater is dark as an eyespot,
      its blank sheet hosts a masquerade,
I spy behind my plastic mask,
          these bichromic glasses,
one row close to my own basilisk.
A strange meeting, he with his obsidian eye,
      me with my wandering gaze.
    These kinds of films count on
one's ability to triangulate the eyes,
      which means nothing for someone like me,
          someone not quite stereoblind.
Cue chromatic blasts, lava red and tropic blue,
      silver-scaled gargoyles leaping
          off the projector screen,
tasteful, waist-up female nudity,
      the fatale femme.
He sees in apple red. I see in dahlia blue,
in pit eye, button eye, the glass eye
of a taxidermy trophy.
    Eye of Provence, Eye of Horus,
where my eyes should trace a triangle shape,
      left eye, right eye, down to mouth,
          instead mine play a game of croquet with wickets
              scattered all around a stranger's head,
                targets I madly whack.
      He sees in apple red, I see in dahlia blue,
    he would slice my eye with a razor through.
Red eye, cyan eye, this begins and ends with the lens.

M@ur!ce Hǝnry's Mannequin

Just shut up and let me think
please—
If I meditate,

will I become marbled
and statuesque?
Or if I medicate, can I stop

the hurricane?
It all goes back
to either my magenta gel pens

or my incarnadine vitamins,
I can't decide.
When I was fifteen, I needed

a left kidney, so I made one
out of clay and papier-mâché.
Now, the faux organ flutters

near my spine, a gauzy wing,
a whirligig spinning.
When I was ten, I collected

different dead insects
and arachnids.
I spread their skeletons

across glossy cardstock pages
with milky modge podge
to make arthropod collages.

Then, when I was three,
a television crushed me.
At the time, all TVs were oblong

plastic boxes, wide like coffins.
Before the screen hit me,
I saw myself briefly in the black glass.

My head was the whole earth.
My scream was soft fog
that had fallen from a larger cloud.

It all stops there.
I had the story straight before,
on the last last day of school,

and once at a mall, and the first time
someone asked me, *When you grow up,
what do you want to be?*

But I got sick of other people
who could not have a thought
without me, and I started therapy.

So just tell me now
—will the rain ever end
if I make up my mind?

Exquisite Corpse #01

a pulse throbs in the throat like a small frog
hemorrhage and shock, a doll served up in a tray

in bleached anemones
the aquamarine ball gown, jellyfish bell
a bralette and a set of dried butterflies

what to be: articulated doll
wanted to be: a woman in a state of reverie
or apparent death,
an artist's jointed model,
dressmaker's figure
one in soliloquy

empty, whole, hidden, closed
made of wicker, made of wire, papier-mâché,

every time a woman dies, P!c@ss° collects her
the rest of the bisected women are in the Louvre now

airbrushed corpse, Neptune moon
the human head weighs eight pounds
her head only, made of stone

wax, plaster, narcissus flower
the voice on the other side of the phone
the body is a temporary way of being
and there are documented messages between dreams

nothing is wasted, not even the pain
of enchanted figurines

Gloria de Herrera, Saint-Martin d'Ardèche, France

I come by my disorder honestly. Nothing appears to be wrong.
My father loved me. He keeps my teeth in a jar on his windowsill.
>Those white scales glare in the pale daylight.
>They are what I was meant to lose.

And nothing appears to be wrong, but there's two of me,
a stupid duality.

>One of me wanders free on seashores and beaches.
>If ever she reaches water, her life will begin,
>that hatchling sea turtle of a girl.
>Until then, she waits for her egg tooth to sprout.
>She only wants to get out of her leather shell.
>I hope she lives.
>
>The other of me? I keep her secret
>on a Mediterranean isle, in a stone Roman prison cell.
>She wears a jade green mask.
>She basks in shadow. She asks for blue sky, a spyglass,
>and to view nine dead butterflies arranged in a tray.
>
>This is what it means to make peace with oneself,
>to live with the person who wants to destroy you.

Nothing appears to be wrong.
My mother offers me my own teeth as though they are hers
to return. And I multiply.

I throw the eggshell delicate girl into a mirror's enameled plane.
The mirror works both ways, the face of the other woman in jade
is splayed across the cursed surface.

                              She and she and I
might have one body, might be one body, who is to say?
We three bleed together in looking glass debris,
                              in those pieces sharp as teeth.

Devouring woman, devouring woman—
                              I know soon she will consume me.

We were predisposed. So it's no one's fault exactly.
I am her sister intrauterine, she is an animal cannibal,
she is a reef shark with embryonic teeth.
                    This disease belongs to she and she and me.

Maybe once I knew, but now I've lost track of who's who,
of the teeth I keep, of the teeth I lose.

The Weaver of Verona

The story told in this painting is obvious: This lady is knitting, is making animate characters that fly out the window.
—Remedios Varo

1.
How did you make it?
Hazel Lakeman, by the spool you looped
lengths of wool. Together the threads began
as white then dispersed
into purple and electric blue,
turned fuchsia, magenta, and red.
You held all the twisting stitches live
on your prismatic needles.
You made the strange rainbow blanket,
your gift to me,
my doing and undoing.

2.
I cannot make it back there,
back to the wool white house
where I am soft as fontanels,

back when my mother hovers
over me. She sees the delicate
places just over my brain.

She laments that I am sensitive
each time I cry before the TV,
that square where cartoon animals

parade, gray-eyed spiders spying
prey, those lost dogs wandering
across mossbound rocks, and rats

as fat as hogs robbing dark, forgotten
county fairs. I swear, I feel everything
I see there. It is as alive as me.

I gather it all in, inside my wide
blanket with me as I press inside
my head. As I suck my thumb,

I make a shape inside me
and find relief, my deep secret.
My mother does not know

what to do with me. I cannot see
myself as she sees me. Still, I wonder
what exactly others me,

what is so deeply wrong with me.
In all these memories,
my rainbow blanket warms me,

it makes my veil, my cape.
It makes me safe.
The square contains

faint traces of where I have been,
my father's arm,
my grandmother's embrace.

And so I discover ways to escape,
to create open space for me.
I cannot make it back there.

But I remember what it is like
under that blanket sky,
with its colors always sunset, sunrise.

That atmosphere is with me,
it endures in rainbow chains,
in cabled rows and hollow hearts.

3.
You said
what I see in my head is not real
as it seems to me,
but listen to this dream.
She is making blankets
out of clouds.
When mine rises up,
yours bows to mine.

4.
The blanket frays.
One heart makes

a blank space,
one makes

a shriek,
a scream,
I dive into.

Rainbow threads pass
over my head.

I don't want to die
now, I want to die

and tell what it is like—
to explain,
to talk back,
to say, *Here,*
this is the blanket you have.
And when you
pass through,
the blanket has you—

Now I pass through.

5.
Hazel Lakeman,
now I am alive in your mind.

While you sit in front of your TV,
your hands move up and down,

two pistons in a death machine.
As you go on weaving,

you are doing and undoing me—
All my days are chains of yarn

slipping through your needles.
You count me off as your niece

counts on giving birth to a girl.
The blanket is for her and for me.

Are we alive at the same time?
What is it like when you die?

My life loops on before me, off
from your great silver sickles.

Each stitch will appear nearly
invisible when you are through

making me the strange rainbow,
chains of wool woven together

some night before you will die
in a car on Mount Hope Road.

When you die you know what waits
latent in the blanket you make,

and how to find relief,
what you weave into empty space.

6.
What else did she lace
there on her spool?
What else did she weave

into each row
with her pair of needles
when she made me

the strange rainbow blanket?
The loops loosened,
and thread she had woven so neat

and narrow grew far apart
and scrawling to create one chain,
like the elongating shapes

handwritten cursive letters make.
When she planned to weave
a gift for me did she leave

other traces? Did she imagine me
in plans she made? Did she see
she and I are of one kind,

of one mind?
I did not mind who I was
when I was a child, I was blank

as light, containing other rays.
And I did not mind the blanket fraying.
It was as Great Aunt Hazel designed.

7.
You said
what I see in my head
is not real,
but listen to this dream:
She is making blankets
out of burial shrouds.

When mine rises up,
it clouds everyone's sun,
it annihilates the sky.

8.
When my mother's scissors glide
against my sky, I am on the other side.

This is the gift she gives
and the gift she takes.

Where can I go? The hole
I pass through passes
through shears then disappears
with me inside.

The strange rainbow rains
its colors over me,
red, gold, orange, and coral—

I am somewhere
beyond her scissor pair
in the blushes of a sunset,
in the handful of threads she severs.

This is how she cures me, a lobotomy.
Her shears tear my eyelet heart wide.

9.
Here a rainbow waits to separate.
Over gray basalt columns and aquamarine hot springs,
above black beaches, or ultramarine and green seas,
in mistblow, in moonglow, rising from the sprays of waves,
submerged below water, merged on water's surface—
each ray is patient, each wave weaves itself through,
is illusion, indigo, blue.
Here a rainbow readies to form,
to be born of light, to transform.

10.
The remains of my strange rainbow
await me. My mother preserves them
inside an antique steamer chest,
deep, chestnut brown, and definite.

I am nearly thirty as she returns
to me what I have long left behind:
old papers with grades in red pen,
blue and ruby competition ribbons,

and small dolls I made from paper-mâché.
I do not ask her why nor by what right
she removes these souvenirs,
all my memories,

from my childhood bedroom.
As she sees it, all these as well as me
are hers in the way one keeps
something one creates. She cannot see

that something else made me.
I am separate.
By now the strange rainbow
has drained. It is a small white square

with one heart inside.
And I remember what it is like
to arrive through the open throat
of the wide threads, to scream,

to sense her scissors slice
inside my head.
If hurting me could cure me
she and I might see eye to eye

because I tried that, too.
But what is wrong with me is inside
the strange rainbow
Hazel Lakeman made me.

11.
Great Hazel,
I unwind your phantom thread.

I will make it back to you
at spectral edge of mind.

Great Hazel, you loom.
You are atmosphere to me.

You weave.
You cast me off your needles.

I rise red, pure carmine,
doing and undoing me.

See the way I contort myself?
See how I will make myself

fit inside this life I have left?
I am your strange rainbow.

I am light, prism, and point of view.
Great Hazel, here I pass through.

Lost Object

Sunset Cliffs, San Diego, California

There and back again, seafoam and white surf turn
        to sawtooth claws, as you dogpaddle straight to G°d.
Here, it's midnight on the other side of the horizon,

        and the sun is a Ferris wheel agleam, it creaks around
        a single cold bolt. It blinks coral, teal, celadon green.

The great wheel, it reels you in by the clear, thin wire
        of your life. Stroke by stroke, the terracotta coast sails
far and farther away from those unstable coastal cliffs,

        cliffs too soft to climb, cliffs off which you lifted,
        from which you jumped into the Pacific to swim.

Listen. Can't you hear the gray whales far below?
        They migrate back to the Bering Sea. And listen—
you can hear the thoughts of cephalopods wander

        as they prod you through water, their tens and tens
        of gentle tentacles egging you along, a swift surface

current. There and back again, you've come to life,
        you can breathe beneath the sea, and you can see
in saline waters. At last, you are as G°d made you

        —an indestructible object. Draw it all in. The dark
        dot of your pupil swells to drain the ink-black sea,

that park ride in the sky, the sun spins in your iris.
        Here, paddle until you find a permeable membrane—
when it rains just so in a dream, it rains on you, too.

  And as you swim you come to know, there's this,
  what you hold in each stroke of your arms, and not

this, what lies on the other side of consciousness.
  Remember? You woke up and recounted a dream,
what you'd seen in your sleep, not this, but beyond,

    then back to this—it was a crystalline river horse
    that smiled with human teeth, the black and white

photograph of Atlantis ruins in which you lived,
  the dress you made of barracuda-blue anemones
and wore to visit the Cote d'Azur. There and back

    again, if you return, you can climb up the cliffs,
    it's possible, the way a memory can pass from life

into dreams and back, and back into other dreams.
  A lover's eye, the morning star haunts the dawn,
it swings across the sky on a silent metronome.

    O come, o come, Ǝmm@nUəl, there and back again.
    There's a dream no one wakes from, none recounts,

G°d looked you straight in the eye and told you so.
  And M@n R@y no longer responds to any inquiries
about the ready-made titled Object to Be Destroyed.

[3]

From Another Approach

Glymur waterfall, Hvalfjörður fjord, Iceland

Here is where earth opens
like a verdigris-green egg,

having kept many secrets so long—
its pumice stone pores,

its silicate tadpoles, moss-damp
and soft for metamorphosis.

Here, floating in the open air,
here, between the ocean and a lake

laced with whale bones, water falls.
So balance on the edge of earthshell

knowing that once the emerald urn
of the earth swallowed water,

its turbid mystery. This was far
away in time, long before

any legend arrived in mind's eye.
Below the perpendicular cliffs

awash with lichen light as ice,
a wool-thick shawl of moss

across black volcanic rock,
a swift river flowing over

stepping stones, a surge
that once churned

below the earth's surface
in those hidden oceans,

alongside other mysteries
of the deep. These columns

called cliffs recall
another secret unearthed here,

the legend of one cursed
creature, once a sailor,

then a whale that chased
innocent fishers from the ocean

to above the falls, where the whale
finally died, not vanquished but exhausted.

And now this is above,
the same place where wide water glides

across the horizon and spills
into the sky, where the water

sharpens the small rocks it keeps
inside itself, each a small secret,

each a harpoon dart artfully carved
to pierce bones in bare feet.

Here is the malachite mountain
where earth opens. The cliff-edge falls

like water, a great cascade, white rain rises,
the light recedes over the edge,

the water droplets stop dropping,
steep overflow, sweet vertigo.

W°lfg@ng P@@lən's Mannequin

                Teal and algal flowering,
the unreal hot spring, the Blue Lagoon
is a bright damselfish swimming
                  among black volcanic rocks.

This is a late stage of her poor metamorphosis
when she is first free of habit,
when she sheds her drab covering,
a young nun bathing in a milky blue pool.

      How many spa visits, how many baptisms
before she reaches the warm shore called healing?

        The myths are unclear about this issue,
describing instead the many golden ornaments
she has already seen rise from other waters,
the hairpins and rings
                that cost others their lives,
the sister who drowned for the gilt comb,
her sister who rode a dappled-gray horse in after.

         Above the aurora glitters like silica,
                all absinthe and ultramarine,
        while she wades the azure acres.

Mythic and blissful, in the cobalt bolt of lake,
the waters take as long as they take, and they take.

Experimental Research

Nocturnal, unfavorable to either love or metamorphosis, the object sits in the palm. Pythagorean, it calls numbers god. It catalogs each day of its life. And it dies if photographed, digitally or on film.

It lives in the open mouth of a nude woman. If she is sleeping, it appears at her throat, where it clutches her neck like a faux-gold choker. And if she were dead? It would rest in the hollow of her pelvis, about twelve inches away from where she'll lay carefully posed, an exsanguinated figurine, an exquisite corpse.

Once it is dead-dead on a dissecting table, if one plays math rock music, it changes like some cacti, the princess of night blooming in moonlight once each decade, when it displays its obscure and brutal beauty.

Exquisite Corpse #04

lobotomize me
reality has a stranglehold
on a life I slept through

where the classic American tragedy
wears Prussian blue on V-J Day
& kisses a sailor in uniform

where any object maker can
draw a line from J@ck the R!ppər
through to the Cubists

making one mark for the artist
who painted Camden Town
one for the Mona Lisa's thief

& one for the death that talked
like priests with doves

the rest is an intellectual game
a suicide note on plastic magnets

M@rcəl DⅬch@mp's Mannequin

Cross the line, thin as a metal hanger.
Say the word—

as a girl, refuse to play the part even in the mind,
abandon once and for all, the crib's bars, wood and wire.

Know there are many garments to hang other than gowns,
an opal-sequin cape, a pilot's uniform,
a mermaid's glamourous clamshell with pearlescent contours.

Outside of want, of right, of loss of any kind,
keep still—the hanger is also a small sword.

Nahui Olín at a Bullfight

you are born under taurus the bull waiting to gore to take sweet girl you are matador listen aureate spectators adore as you wave your roseate cape you are born under taurus the ring a warped iris is yours as you cow in the bull's gaze sweet girl you are matador and yet you pity the bull/mourn you who you cannot escape you are born under taurus hoof you/r disorder perform nurture/nature it's simple fate sweet girl you are matador so give what the crowd paid for face the bull its ancient rage you are born under taurus sweet girl you are matador

The Lovers

Darling, this is all wrong, I cannot look you in your obsidian eye.

Only bed sheets keep us apart, you and I are lost in soft cotton,
moonstone glow, and pearl white, a secret on display.

Now this is as close as you and I can ever get to love,
I never press my skin to yours, or you, yours to mine,
but this is more than you and I will never have, not less.

So, Darling, why do you pull this cloth against my face so tight?

Yv∂s T@ngⅡy's Mannequin

For one last look, turn back to the room.
                                         It is all gone,

somnambulant hairpins rest on a plastic mat long-packed,
         and the half-scrap receipts, and the blank bank statements,
the notes you wrote in your own hand on the sides of envelopes,
         a password you scratched out, a four-digit pin.
Even the bedsheets evaporated, moisture and mist.

Nothing is missing. So what good is it to ask—
         Would you stay? If you could?

Dust collects in the vacuum canister,
         earth from your shoes, soil in the air,
particles of skin, a bit of you.
         And so you give the room one last look.

°sc@r D°m!ngU∂z's Mannequin

                I made the odyssey of turtles
in August, by the eye-blue promenade,
              with espadrilles in hand.

       This was after I rose up the Rock of Monaco,
after the blush pink medieval alleys
where I walked as quiet as a friar,
     after the castle with its dole of oddities—

      a wood pod submersible,
                a gyroscopic table,
the black tooth of a megalodon,

     and the Adriatic seaweed,
white baleen bones, dark octopus beaks,
        the pennate skeletons of manta rays,
        and fluorescent corals.

     What remained salient for me was the sanctuary,
that temporary heaven for indestructible objects,
   where turtles swam in a saltwater veranda.

They were patient as angels behind a glass edge,
with their sea in view over the travertine ledge.

And the Mediterranean was a lazuli haze,
   the stones of the beach were carapace gray,
each was fixed as a sea turtle shell,
   as I stepped off the angel walk into the sea.

The Vet and the Bull

She reached the absence. She came on all fours before it. Still, its surface went on annihilating light, absorbing as though porous, an infinite sponge. All was spare there, all excess, all lack, of a kind with the famine in her mind. By the care of the strange aids in that black, she achieved anesthesia. Neither the adipocere snake nor the black-caped songbird overheard her backwards count when they bathed her in peppermint, juniper, myrrh, when they swabbed her with a balm of decapitated carnations. And, blacked out, she never saw God enter in, clean and beaming, ready to perform for the aseptic operating theater, spotlit and spotlight. Her thoughtful doctor, her surgeon, he left his lancet inside her, deep. So she would maintain every memory of her own trepanation. Afterward, the aids painted forms on her: a score of enormous aurochs in ochre iron oxide and the ancient constellation Taurus. They remade her more mortal than before. They cast her in silver. She shined like a scalpel.

[4]

Ǝsp!n°z@'s Mannequin

Take me, for instance, and what I must have known
about the aluminum spoons in the silverware drawer,
and the cut grass on the lawn weaving upon itself,
those blades interlaced like fingers on clasped hands.

I was one of four, or often five, in our warm house
without any cupboard, or a square washer to hum,
without a dryer to knead clothes like bread dough,
warm and wet. In the sitting room, where we met,

office chairs lined white walls, and blank diaries
waited to collect our thoughts, those papers empty
as our strange warm house with its quiet rooms,
each an open square as wide as a calendar page.

I arrived hypothermic, but I believed no cold could
touch either me or the false heat that kept me alive.
It isn't possible to know how I brought myself there.
I had been living among the tombs on the other side

of the sea. I had opened myself with small stones.
It was a kind of possession until those spirits left,
when I came back to my right mind in that room.
In a circle, we spoke about what brought us there,

the ways we played as small children, of the care
and feeding of horses, the record-keeping of tides.
We spoke in turns, warming the air with our breath,
each breath which in turn mixed with the earthly

mystery of how we each arrived. Take Golconda,
take sweet Aurora, and small Rosemond. Inside
that house, they locked their names like jewels
in a squat safe, winding and unwinding its dial

until all the small numbers and scores fell away
from the circle, spinning and shimmering bright.
In our circle, they each fell away, too, their voices
were small values, quiet clicks or taps to which one

presses one's ear to listen because meaning is there
somewhere, within a quick and irregular rhythm.
They were there with me, so what does it matter
that none of us could ever say quite how we came

to crowd the house with our obsessed presences?
In our house, a circle widened, closed, and opened
again, and under our shuffling feet the floorboards
creaked. Our cracked saucers clinked like silver

coins as we sipped from chipped cups. And sudden
gusts outside trembled the window's lead weights
and called to something still frozen inside Salomé,
so she would swell the great blanket that enveloped

her like a frothing wave. And yet it does matter how.
In me there was legion. So how did I move? No one
could approach us outside the tombs. Was I moved?
Where does one spirit end? Or another spirit begin?

These are the questions of any physical possession.
So then how? I ask because at the end somehow
I came to sit in that warm room, that second womb,
where I would try to understand the strange cries

rising over the steep embankment of a distant sea,
on those nights as I sat there in my square chair,
my hands clasped in my lap, at special attention
resembling prayer. I ask because the way down

any road feels slower than the way back, even if
the distance doesn't change. I ask so I can find
my own way back, even slowly, even in the dark.
And so I hold to what I wrote on one cold night:

It is so sad to sit and hear the things the boy feels.
But those are the things that brought us all here.
Small Golconda, little brother, your breath appears
here in the air. It is a thin mist, but it is true enough

to collect in a spoon, as true as the combination
to a lost lock, true as small stones the sea smooths
so soft they no longer hurt, true as an open window,
as the small square where cold and warm air collide.

Girl with Death Mask

Joshua Tree National Park, Twentynine Palms, California

She pictures the boulder they call skull, then her eyes close.

That grotesque head calls from the wonderland of rocks,
from among twisting granite monoliths
and other stones as sharp as bone shards,
from beyond the lost palms that grace a salt-white oasis,
beyond dust-hills the sun's rush colors almond and ochre,
beyond the arid garden square where yellow-green chollas grow.
That is one desert, where her thought is only water.
This is another.

Desert of thought, consciousness lost on the operating table,
her body is a copper mine long forgotten, and her head rests
in the hands of surgeons unearthing a tumor.

Rock of the brain, a patient rain hollows holes in stone.
Head in the desert, she returns there with a skull eroded.

X-ray of My Skull

Hold still, the room is bone-white,
            the radiograph is ready.

Before the first X-ray was made,
        there was a wife. This tradition
is made in her image.
      Before I was anyone's wife, I was a girl.
Before I was a girl, I was a wave of light.
I still remember what it is like
      to move through,
to pass through objects and softer tissues.

What I am doing now is as close
as I have been to that way of movement
because I am telling the truth:

      there is you, who I promise myself to,
and there is not you.
I am true to both, both can be true.

My lungs, my heart, these are shadows
on a luminescent screen. My bones are light.
I have nothing to hide. It is true.
      The first X-ray was of a wife.
She lay her hand between ray and plate.
    And in the faint green light of the screen,
her ring became opaque to the rays.

M@n R@y's Mannequin

Saguaro National Park West, Tucson, Arizona

Do not look, and do not look away—
halogen bright, a late-night drive,
at the end of the world, the horizon

passed its light pink tourmaline beads
from one hourglass half to the other,
leaving one bulb hollow, nebula blue.

On the stereo, a woman retells a time
another woman died, a brutal crime,
a cold case to keep one up at night.

Animal eyes shine from the roadside,
pairs of honeycombs and marigolds,
in and out of the quartz iodine gleam.

The pickup truck in red-rock canyons
is a shriek in the night, either the cry
of a woman in peril or the careful call

of a predator in disguise. However brief,
there is everything in high beams' reach,
and everything else, everything hidden

just on the other side of the dark, velvet
ash and sycamore, and more eyes—rose
quartz and meadowsweet, sargassum

seagrass and moons of mars aglow
while mars observes earth, sky-side
in outer space. It's background sound

on an unscenic drive, the tragic myth
of the mannequin woman. Her life,
however brief, flashed like a halogen

beam, so the talk show host covered
everything else, the desert at night.
In a pair of eyes, one eye is the sun,

the other is the moon, mascara lining
each, dark aura in the early morning.
On the road, a set of headlights arrive,

and light creeps in at first, then burns
into view and explodes. Like shrapnel
it passes through the eyes, then embeds

itself deep within the brain, remaining
in sight even after eyes close, one sun,
one moon, while the stereo drones on.

Portrait of Space

                      So the outcome—
the mosquito net recreates a nameless shape,
the mirror hangs there barely, almost falling
      from its invisible hook.

     Tell me, will you keep them?
      The silver shears, what you use
to cut into that last atmosphere,
the veil you looked through so long.
       That unbelievable blue is gone,
      and pure azure is long off.

And look at you, alone
in what you made, and maybe
         a little lonesome in the aftermath.
Afterall, you were accustomed to the view.
Afterall, you knew who you were
      behind the thousand careful squares
          of your protective screen.

In this place, in the vacant landscape,
there are many ways to view what you made.
        It is a white dove,
    a kiss soft on the cheek,
a cirrus cloud misting into oblivion.
          But a cloud making the shape
of anything is still water blotting the sky.

         So, tell me, if you know,
   now that it's over,
      what good is it, all this, open?

The Years Lie in Wait for You

On every stone a petroglyph,
               a wheel, a snake, a star.
      They are cut together,
they blink through film projector eye.

      In white clay, selenite, and bone,
in whirlpool curls, in hurricane turns,
        on the sheet-screen,
the images reel until the images unreal.

In mineral, an etch, a groove, a score of earth,
in skin, a crease of the hand, a line at the eye,

one does not catch the pictures flicker,
        nor silk web depart the spinneret.

From lamp to film to lens, the light,
from mind to hand to stone, the relief—

On every stone a petroglyph,
        and under every stone a spring,
                silent, cold, and coiling.

Minotaur

                        You ask, Where does it go?

Back to the white-snow abyss I conjure like an old habit
as easy for the brain as breathing.

Yes, I tried the cures. In French ultramarine,
I watercolored the angel walk on the Côte d'Azur,
I masked myself in black mud, in sulfur and salt,
then waded at midnight into the Blue Lagoon—

                        but the lust returns.
No matter how many pearlescent sugar pills you swallow,
or X-marked eggs you turn in their incubator womb,
that way of loving will not leave the body.

It beats like a slow pulse, once a second or less.
It recalls cold nights inside me, our unspeakable art.

Slow love in the head, I was not strong enough to stop
my hair from breaking, in black and brown and white.
I cracked like a bone, my thoughts burned like ice.

In this way, I held myself, centerfold and creased,
feeling, as a creature from some other distant star,
the elemental weight of air, when all left was breath.

The edge of breath—this, all by itself,
offers a scarce and quiet joy, delighting in me,
if I can get there, if I can get back.

In soaked wool, with lips blue and limbs numb,
I am cold through the marrow.
For miles, it promises the only open door.

    It is a love as simple as wanting to be warm.

Exquisite Corpse #05

        this is what I worked out in secret
     gravity is part of the falls
flame devours vapor to make the light

        now my passport is blank
    so is the ancient map

I folded on its even creases
   thin troughs soft as riverbeds

     geothermal steam rises around me
from earth, a vapor like sunrise
as delicate, as brief

     by this river, down this path
I've been running barefoot,
   like how we used to swim then
when we were small children

     leaping in tumbling seas
     our salt-wet skin glinting like scales

then, when we were secretless
creatures content in their make believe play
     daughters of the water swimming
with mermaids in the waves

this is what I worked out in secret
     we have never been as much as we are
     we have more to be because we are here

Observatory Time, the Lovers

*The women that are sketched backwards are
the only ones that have never been seen*
   —André Breton, "The Enchanted Well"

That fracture cracked into a pale fish-scale sky, your mouth
is starlet-scarlet, cadmium, crimson, carmine—a red ravine.

How halcyon, the view in my mind's eye.
      Blue sky, I mine what it might mean,
            I mine red. Day by day, I bleed
               your lips across a canvas wide and white,
      three feet high and eight feet from side to side.

      I have to draw you.
I have to draw you forth, the reservoir
               of memory is my sole source,
the wellspring that weeps, that open sore.
      To make you, I have torn a score
            of metal ores across the blade
of my palette knife, the clay and rib
                  from which I form your lips.

   Your lips, they eclipse the sky, that vast overcast vault,
pillow light, smoke white, and laced with cruel cerulean.

                  Mine is a horizon with no sun.
Of course, once there was a sun, a red dwarf one,
until I lined the sky with ladders,
      then I climbed and climbed.
            That scarlet star was ripe,
               an open fracture, a cracked bone
I brought up to my mouth, to my blood-plump lips.

Imagine, if you can, what it's like to consume a star—
     crumbling sponge cake in red velvet,
          burning current of currant jam,
              strawberries carved into playing card hearts,
and a handful of cherries each complete with its pit.

    Bite by bite, I consumed the sun.
And after I peeled that orb apart,
     what remained pooled
in a rough red rind, all dust and dew.
       So I took a plastic straw, striped white and blue,
       and I sucked those million vermillion filaments
out of the very husk of dusk.
I devoured the blush of the sun,
I exsanguinated the sky
     while the observatory tower cowered
           in the blank atmosphere.
    It was a sight to behold.
         If only you had been there.

Somewhere, elsewhere, you bled, you bleed.
I search for you in the widening sky of time.

And so I lay here bare in a black bed of velvet.
       There is a chess board at my feet,
    a feminine bend to my knees,
    and my taut torso forms a cupid's bow.
    Your mouth hangs over me.
And unless I close my eyes,
my gaze remains on your lips in my sky.
I face away,

            a muse, I bare nothing,
                        I bare everything.
I lay naked yet take the photograph.
            And my rouge ruse, how amusing,
this photograph is black and white.
            Mind you, there's something here
                        in how still I manage to hold back,
in how I rely on this—the lack.

In harsh-charcoal, platinum, ash, and stone,
                        your lips are my apocalypse,

a last crevasse of scaled-back black.
How bleak, a flash, a reverie.
            Gray sky, I mine iron.
                        I mind where you might be. I have to—
                        I have to draw. I have to draw you forth,
                        my soul, my open sore.

This piece is a photograph of you and me.
It's me as much as you,
            the clot that blots the maroon and oozing wound,
                        the checked board on which rests
                        a chess set of geometric forms,
the light-bending lenses and recessed refracting glass
            the observatory telescope possesses.
It's true. Some objects come into view
            only with others in the way.

        It's you, it's me.
       I consumed the sun.
It's me, let me exhume you from the crush.
       Your lips drift over me.
           It's me, my dear departed.
             I am art and artist.

The sky is an azure tide,
      your mouth a red cyclamen scythe.
          The night is wide. It spreads,
a tender bruise in midnight blue.
A bloodshot comet with no predictable return,
       you recur in my dreams.
    Some nights, your lips shed petals,
you shower me with incarnate carnations,
      gargantuan chrysanthemums,
          and cotton-soft cosmos flowers.
             Darling, I hasten the hour of your return,
    the minute at the limit of your endurance,
    the moment when the word you've wanted long

        is on the tip of my tongue.
       Darling, I'm so close, it's on my lips—
           And for the rest? I'll not speak of it.

       Cadmium and crimson fade
    to charcoal, ash, and stone.
    I lie alone, poised to bring you back,
          posed to withhold.
Who can know
if I keep my eyes open or closed? You,
    I picture you, I picture I look up at you—

     —if only you were here.
    I am the sight to behold.

You are red lips in my sky, the blood-sly smile
I lie beneath bare, at once aware

    the color carmine contains two drops of blue,
  at once a dream, my lips colored a sapphire hue.

Siren Stars Alice

from Sophie Puchulu | ♪ @squishiesophie2

My cure came at night. But that is coincidence,
pure and stark as stars.

> *When I was in the mental hospital,*
> *the only thing I did was make paper stars.*

On my first visit, the nurse gave me pen and paper
so I could learn to make a work like hers,
a meadow starred with flowers.
My pages were as blank as me, vacant
except for bright blue rules.
When I tried to outline what I had in mind,
my meadow scene was something else entirely—
deep wide-open space.
Still, I liked what I was trying.

> *So I spent twelve to sixteen hours every day*
> *just making paper stars.*
> *There was this one girl,*
> *and she would steal some of my paper stars.*
> *She'd sit next to me and put them in her pocket.*
> *But I continued to make the paper stars.*

I practiced my craft in different shapes,
until I landed on small pentagons.
I learned to take my pen against the paper,
making long, straight lines,
left to right, low to high. That was when my pages changed
and became papers full of stars.

> *I was there for one week, and then I got let out.*

A hundred hours passed by, tiny satellites
burning out under the night.

> *What did I do with my new freedom?*
> *I made more paper stars.*

I learned to make them by habit. And I kept filling pages.

> *I kept making paper stars.*
> *I made them until my fingers were sore,*
> *I made them until I could no longer fold the paper.*

Sometime, my eyes went blue as the dye of lines,
and my head took on the shape of a pentagon.
Eventually, I saw the night was full with stars
I had been making.
Each star gave away to another star,
then each star gave itself away.
They had been rising all that time,
like so many flowers sprouting out from earth,
a bright meadow in the sky, making light,
creating new constellations alongside so many other stars,
each handworked, handspun, handmade.

> *And then after all of that, I made more paper stars.*

Given: 1. The Waterfall, 2. The Illuminating Gas

           —For me, it was a resurrection.
Like all the rest of you, I moved through the humid

air of youth as well as I could, with two spinal discs
fused, with a metal rod metacarpal, with a prosthetic

foot in one shoe.
           Like you, I am here because I live,

which, you understand, is not a simple consequence
for one like me. There were so many nights I posed

with my hands together, open, and ready to receive
one token of relief, an aluminum spoon, a smoothed

stone or empty shell, a single indigo butterfly wing.
And there were times I came quite close to holding

life in my hand's palm, not all, but certainly a part.
Some of it all, and not because I was less. Instead,

I unrolled myself. I was an ocean, dim and abysmal.
And it all came in—in polluted pools, in saccharine

potions, in iridescent poisons and soured antidotes.
I learned to drink up any water I saw, in the grottos

of underworldly blue, from bases of aging glaciers,
from acrid outer seas, all sunstone green and saline.

But I swear, I had some of it all,
                        in teal arctic caves,

in toy pianos practicing complex melancholy songs,
in basalt columns alongside jet black silica beaches,

in some museums, and in those museums, in rooms
behind strange doors made for one to look through.

I had some, and perhaps you had more,
                                    more of life

to add to mine, and mine to yours. And if I am here,
it is to be a breaker in the deluge, in the water chute

I plunge my bare arm through, that moving tableau,
and it is to carry air, that spare and elemental vapor,

and call that atmosphere to light, then light to sight,
because whatever I did not make, I will be adding to,

the dripping wick thick with kerosene, the light mist
rising from water, rocks, and moss. All this follows

from what I have been given, the rest is left for you.
And you can call it what you will—a gift, a promise,

a burden, or a curse. For me, it was uncircumscribed
and quiet, an old lantern burning, a resurging spring

hidden within earth's obsidian and infinite fissures.
I came to life for this—

Notes

To varying degrees, the poems in this collection reference works by Surrealist artists. All artworks are listed by artist.

André Masson. *Mannequin by André Masson.* International Exhibition of Surrealism, Paris, 1938.

Espinoza. *Mannequin by Espinoza.* International Exhibition of Surrealism, Paris, 1938.

Denise Bellon, Gala Dalí, Nusch Eluard, and Yolande Oliviero. "Experimental Research: On the Irrational Knowledge of the Object: The Crystal Ball of the Seers." *Le Surréalisme ASDLR no. 6* (May 1933).

Dora Maar. *The Years Lie in Wait for You.* 1936.

Dorothea Tanning. "Septième péril (Seventh Peril)" from *Les 7 périls spectraux (The Seven Spectral Perils).* 1950.

Emmy Bridgewater, Ithell Colquhoun, Irène Hamoir, and Edith Rimmington, "Surrealist Inquiry: What Do You Hate the Most?" *Savior vivre*, edited by René Magritte, (1946).

Frida Kahlo. *Girl With Death Mask (She Plays Alone).* 1938.

Joan Miró. *Mannequin by Joan Miró.* International Exhibition of Surrealism, Paris, 1938.

Kay Sage. *From Another Approach.* 1944.

Kurt Seligmann. *Mannequin by Kurt Seligmann.* International Exhibition of Surrealism, Paris, 1938.

Lee Miller. *Portrait of Space or Untitled.* 1937.
Tanja Ramm under a bell jar. 1930.

Léo Malet. *Mannequin by Léo Malet.* International Exhibition of Surrealism, Paris, 1938.

Leonora Carrington. *The vet and the bull,* 1951.

Man Ray. *Mannequin by Man Ray.* International Exhibition of Surrealism, Paris, 1938.
Minotaure (Minotaur). ca. 1933.
Object to Be Destroyed. 1923, remade 1933, editioned replica 1965.
Observatory Time, The Lovers (Photograph). 1936.
Resurrection des Mannequins (Resurrection of the Mannequins). 1966.

Marcel Duchamp. *Étant donnés: 1. La chute d'eau, 2. Le gaz d'éclairage (Given: 1. The Waterfall, 2. The Illuminating Gas).* 1946–1966.
Mannequin by Marcel Duchamp. International Exhibition of Surrealism, Paris, 1938.

Marcel Jean. *Mannequin by Marcel Jean.* International Exhibition of Surrealism, Paris, 1938.

Maurice Henry. *Mannequin by Maurice Henry.* International Exhibition of Surrealism, Paris, 1938.

Max Ernst. *Mannequin by Max Ernst.* International Exhibition of Surrealism, Paris, 1938.

Meret Oppenheim. *X-ray of My Skull.* 1964.

Migishi Kōtarō. *Sea and Sunshine.* 1934.

Nahui Olín. *Nahui Olín en una corrida de toros (Nahui Olín at a Bullfight).* Oil on wood, Acervo Museo Estudio Diego Rivera, INBA Collection.

Okanoue Toshiko. *Yobi-goe (The Call).* 1954.

Óscar Domínguez. *Decalcomania with River and Bridge.* 1937.
Mannequin by Óscar Domínguez. International Exhibition of Surrealism, Paris, 1938.

Photographer unknown. *Gloria de Herrera, Saint-Martin d'Ardèche, France.* ca. 1950s.

Remedios Varo. *The Weaver of Verona,* 1956.

René Magritte. *Les Amants (The Lovers).* 1928.

Salvador Dalí. *Mannequin by Salvador Dalí.* International Exhibition of Surrealism, Paris, 1938.

Sonia Mossé. *Mannequin by Sonia Mossé.* International Exhibition of Surrealism, Paris, 1938.

Stella Snead. *Ecstatic Cow.* 1943.

Suzanne Muzard, Elsie Houston, and Jeannette Ducrocq Tanguay. "Surrealist Games." "Surrealism in 1929" by *Variétès.*

The Game of Marseille. *Siren Stars Alice.* 1941.

Wolfgang Paalen. *Mannequin by Wolfgang Paalen.* International Exhibition of Surrealism, Paris, 1938.

Yves Tanguy. *Mannequin by Yves Tanguy.* International Exhibition of Surrealism, Paris, 1938.

About the Author

Ruth Towne is the author of *So the Sadness Could Not Hurt* (Kelsay Books, 2025). She is a graduate of the University of Southern Maine's Stonecoast MFA.

Her poetry has appeared in *Holy Gossip, The Lily Poetry Review, Decadent Review, New Feathers Anthology, Coffin Bell Journal, New Note Poetry, In Parentheses,* and the *Stonecoast Review*'s Staff Spotlight. Her poetry has also appeared in Stanford's *Mantis: A Journal of Poetry, Criticism, and Translation*. Her poem "So the Sadness Could Not Hurt" received the second-place Grantchester Award from *The Orchards Poetry Journal*. Her poem "S@lv@d°r D@l!'s Mannequin," published in *BAM Quarterly*, was nominated for the 2025 Best of the Net Anthology.

www.ingramcontent.com/pod-product-compliance
Lightning Source LLC
Chambersburg PA
CBHW072048160426
43197CB00014B/2682